E is for Enchantment

A New Mexico Alphabet

Written by Helen Foster James and Illustrated by Neecy Twinem

Text Copyright © 2004 Helen Foster James
Illustration Copyright © 2004 Neecy Twinem

Sleeping Bear Press™

315 E. Eisenhower Parkway, Ste. 200
Ann Arbor, MI 48108
www.sleepingbearpress.com

© 2005 Sleeping Bear Press is an imprint of Gale, a part of Cengage Learning.

10 9 8 7 6 5

Library of Congress Cataloging-in-Publication Data

James, Helen Foster, 1951-
E is for enchantment : a New Mexico alphabet / written by Helen Foster
James ; illustrated by Neecy Twinem.
p. cm.
ISBN 978-1-58536-153-3
1. New Mexico—Juvenile literature. 2. English language—Alphabet—
Juvenile literature. I. Twinem, Neecy. II. Title.
F796.3.J36 2004
978.9—dc22   2004006090

Printed by China Translation & Printing Services Limited, Guangdong
Province, China. 5th printing. 11/2009

*For my husband Bob, and with sincere appreciation to
Pam Muñoz Ryan and Barbara McNally.*

HELEN

✎

*With love to my enchanted New Mexico,
full of all of my fantastic friends.*

NEECY

A a

Anasazi (an-uh-SAH-zee) is a Navajo Indian word meaning "the ancient ones." They lived almost two thousand years ago on *mesas* (Spanish for a hill with steep sides and a flat top) and canyon cliffs. Their villages were like apartment complexes with hundreds of people living together. They hunted, and they planted beans, corn, and squash.

Anthropologists study pottery, baskets, and other objects the Anasazi left behind to learn more about them. Today you can visit Aztec Ruins National Monument, Bandelier National Monument, and Chaco Culture National Historical Park (a World Heritage Site) to see places where they once lived. They abandoned their homes over 700 years ago. Where they went and why they left is still a mystery.

A is for the Ancient Ones
who long ago in history,
abandoned homes, now crumbling ruins,
and left us with a mystery.

B for famous Smokey Bear, a black bear from our state. You'll see his picture everywhere on signs that educate.

Prevent Forest Fires!

In 1950 a forest fire in the Lincoln National Forest frightened a little black bear cub, and he climbed a tree to escape. He was rescued by firefighters, nursed back to health, and named Smokey Bear. He became a national symbol for fire prevention. His picture reminds all of us to be careful with fire. Smokey Bear Historical State Park in Capitan is dedicated to forest conservation.

Black bears are not always black. They can be black, brown, blonde, or even white. The female is called a "sow," and the male is a "boar." A group of bears is a "sloth" or "pack." The black bear was selected as the state animal in honor of Smokey Bear.

b B

C is for Carlsbad Caverns,
discovered by cowboy Jim White.
This amazing maze of limestone caves
is truly an awesome sight.

Carlsbad Caverns National Park contains one of the world's largest cave systems. It was formed millions of years ago by acidic water carving through limestone. Dripping water left bits of minerals, which built into huge and unusual formations. Native Americans knew about it long ago, but in 1901 a cowboy found the caves when he noticed thousands of bats and went to investigate.

Today there are miles of surveyed caves, but not all of the caverns have been explored. Visitors can tour about three miles of this World Heritage Site. Just like Jim White, visitors are still amazed to see thousands of Mexican free-tail bats leave the caves at dusk to feed on insects.

Storyteller dolls combine the Native American traditions of making pottery and storytelling. Helen Cordero, a Cochiti Pueblo potter, combined these two arts and created the first storyteller doll in 1964. It was a clay grandfather with his mouth wide open and five children on his lap. She made it to honor her own grandfather, a storyteller. Since that first one, these storytellers have become very popular. Now many artists make them in different styles.

Native Americans have been making pottery bowls and decorative pieces for hundreds of years. Maria Martinez was a famous potter from San Ildefonso Pueblo and was known for her black-on-black pottery. She encouraged other Native Americans to practice the arts of their ancestors. Her work can be seen in museums throughout the world.

D for the storyteller Doll
created out of clay
with children gathered on her lap
to hear what she will say.

E e

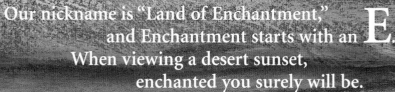
Our nickname is "Land of Enchantment,"
and Enchantment starts with an E.
When viewing a desert sunset,
enchanted you surely will be.

"The Land of Enchantment" is our nickname and it welcomes visitors to see historical and natural sights, interesting wildlife, and enjoy new experiences. What makes New Mexico enchanting? Maybe it's a first visit to one of our Native American reservations to attend a pow-wow. Perhaps it's the fragrance of a piñon pine burning in a fireplace or the sound of a coyote's evening serenade.

New Mexico has enchanting views. In 1924 the Gila Wilderness became the world's first designated wilderness. Gila National Forest is one of the largest national forests in the United States and covers 3.3 million acres. People frequently comment on New Mexico's vast, blue sky. At night, away from city lights, countless stars are visible in the clear, dark sky. For the highest view, Wheeler Peak is the spot, at 13,161 feet above sea level.

All of these and much more combine to make New Mexico "The Land of Enchantment."

It's easy to make a list of favorite foods that are popular in our state. You'll want to try Indian fry bread fresh from a roadside stand or at a special event. Some people put honey on it for a delicious treat.

Enchiladas are a scrumptious combination of sauce, cheese, chiles, onions, and meat rolled in a tortilla. Each year Las Cruces has a "Whole Enchilada Fiesta" to make (and eat!) the world's largest enchilada. (*Fiesta* means party in Spanish.)

The *biscochito* (biz-co-CHEE-toh) was adopted as the state cookie in 1989, making New Mexico the first state to have an official cookie. It is a shortbread cookie with anise flavor and is a favorite at celebrations.

Even our state's official tree makes its way into a meal. Cooks add pine nuts from the piñon tree (or nut tree) to salads, soups, and sauces. It takes about 1,500 tiny nuts to weigh one pound, and a fast picker picks 20 pounds a day.

F is for Indian Fry bread—
on my list as a Favorite Food.
If you made a list of your favorites,
which foods would you like to include?

G for the Glory and Glittering Gold
wanted by Spanish explorers of old.
They journeyed here a long time ago
and named our land "New" Mexico.

Spanish explorers came to present-day New Mexico in the 1500s. They conquered the territory of Mexico, and then they came northward. In 1540 Francisco Vásquez de Coronado led 1,100 men in search of the legendary golden riches of the Seven Cities of Cibola. Native Americans had never seen horses or men in armor with swords or guns. They thought the explorers used "canes that spit fire and made thunder." The Spanish did not find gold and returned to Mexico disappointed, but they claimed the land for Spain and called it *"Nuevo"* Mexico or "New" Mexico.

New Mexico shares an international border with Mexico. It is a bilingual state with two languages recognized by the state's constitution: English and Spanish. One out of three families speak Spanish in their home.

Albuquerque hosts the world's largest Balloon Fiesta. Visitors come every October to see more than 700 colorful balloons rise into the calm morning sky. Balloons operate through the basic principle of hot air rising. A hot air balloon rises when the air inside it is heated. As the air inside the balloon cools, it descends (it comes down). A balloon's pilot can steer a balloon by adjusting its altitude. Pilots like to fly in the early morning because that's when winds are usually the calmest. Gas balloons became part of the event in 1981. A gas balloon is completely enclosed and is filled with helium or hydrogen. Balloons may be unusual shapes such as a flower, stagecoach, pumpkin, dragon, or almost anything you can imagine.

The first balloon flight with passengers was made in 1783 in France. The balloon carried a sheep, a duck, and a rooster. The flight was made in the presence of King Louis XIV and Marie Antoinette. Since that time, people have enjoyed bird's-eye views while riding in a hot air balloon.

H is for Hot Air Balloons
that rise high in the sky.
See their colors and funny shapes.
Come and watch them sailing by.

I is for Inscription Rock,
it soars 200 feet.
For pioneers it meant fresh water
and welcome shelter from the heat.

Ii

Inscription Rock (also called *El Morro*, "The Bluff") is a massive sandstone bluff that rises 200 feet. It's in the El Morro National Monument. The bluff was a welcome landmark for long-ago travelers. It had a reliable waterhole at its base and also grass and shelter. While they rested in the shade, the Spanish explorers and later American pioneers carved messages into the stone including names and dates.

New Mexico has many fascinating rock formations. Shiprock looks like a ship in full sail. Navajos call it Tse' Bit'a'i (The Winged Rock) and consider it a sacred place.

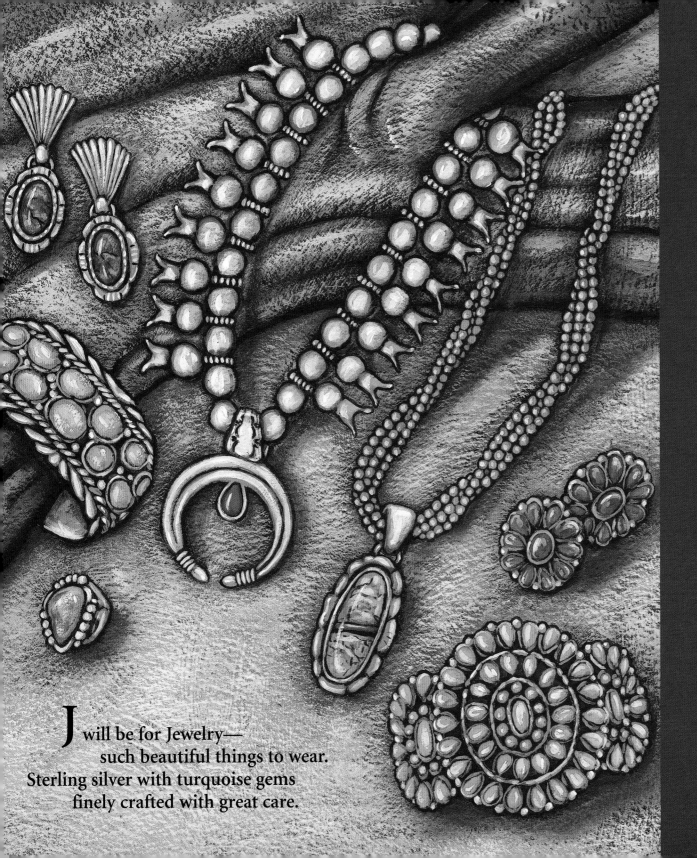

Jewelry from New Mexico is known and prized throughout the world. It is made from various materials including turquoise and silver. Native Americans have a long tradition of making jewelry. They learned silversmithing techniques from Spanish and Mexican silver workers.

Turquoise has been mined in New Mexico for over 1,200 years. It is prized for its beauty and some people think it has the power to make something or someone attractive. It is often used as a symbol for sky. Turquoise is December's birthstone and the state's official gem. It appears in many variations of color from sky blue to green.

The Millicent Rogers Museum in Taos exhibits a collection of historic jewelry collected by Millicent Rogers. She lived in an adobe house in Taos and collected beautiful Native American jewelry and textiles. The museum showcases more than a thousand pieces of jewelry of the Southwest.

J will be for Jewelry—
such beautiful things to wear.
Sterling silver with turquoise gems
finely crafted with great care.

K k

Let's make K for Kokopelli,
a figure scratched upon a rock.
With other ancient petroglyphs,
these rock carvings seem to talk.

Centuries ago people scratched and pecked symbols onto hard rough rocks by striking the surface with a stone or other sharp tool. These rock carvings are called "petroglyphs." The term comes from two Greek words meaning, "rock" and "carving" or "engraving." Rocks can't really talk, but petroglyphs can tell us many things. No one can be certain of the meaning of a particular petroglyph and why it was made. Only the carver really knew. Some were made to tell stories, record events, or even mark a trail. We can admire them for their beauty, and we must respect and protect them for all to enjoy.

A flute player figure, sometimes known as Kokopelli, has been a popular symbol in the Southwest for over a thousand years. Native Americans have many stories about him traveling from village to village, sharing stories, singing songs, bringing seeds, and gathering rain clouds with his flute music.

You'll find thousands of petroglyphs to enjoy at Petroglyph National Monument.

In the 1940s, Los Alamos was the location for a top-secret scientific project. It was here that the first atomic bomb was designed and built. A team of brilliant scientists, engineers, and others, headed by physicist Robert Oppenheimer, worked together in this gigantic effort. Their location and the project were kept secret, even to their relatives and close friends. The nuclear age began when the world's first atomic bomb was tested on July 16, 1945, at Trinity Site, now part of the White Sands Missile Range. The project at Los Alamos brought an end to World War II.

New Mexico is still a leader in space and nuclear energy research. Los Alamos National Laboratory is now an international science think tank where scientists continue research in bioscience, energy, environment, national defense, and space.

Ll

L is for Los Alamos
where scientists work to find
the secrets of atomic worlds
to benefit mankind.

M is for Missions—some big and some small.
Many are short, while others are tall.
Stately and high or humble and low,
all of them treasured by people we know.

An artist might look at one of our missions and see its beauty, while an historian might think of the mission's 400 years of history and its Spanish influence.

Some missions are now in ruins, while many beautiful missions remain and are still in use. San Miguel Mission in Santa Fe is thought to have been built in 1610. This small adobe building is the oldest mission still in use in the United States. Twenty-one thousand adobe bricks were used in its construction. El Santuario de Chimayó is a legendary shrine valued for its healing earth. Artists like to paint pictures of these beautiful buildings that seem brushed by the earth.

M
m

N is for Natural Resources
of copper and uranium ore,
and glistening gypsum crystals
in dunes on the desert floor.

N n

The White Sands National Monument is a unique desert of rare gypsum crystals. The shifting dunes can be 60 feet high and are constantly changing. They grow, crest, slump, and advance driven by the wind. A few plants and animals have been able to adapt to this harsh environment. Gypsum is used to make many products, but the National Monument is protected so visitors will always be able to enjoy its unique natural beauty.

New Mexico has an abundance of other natural resources. Paddy Martinez, a Navajo Indian, found uranium ore while herding sheep one day in 1950. Today New Mexico is a leading uranium-mining state. Uranium is used to generate energy and for medical uses. New Mexico is also a source of potash (used to make fertilizer), copper, petroleum, and natural gas. Our other natural resources include animals, forests, grasses, and plants.

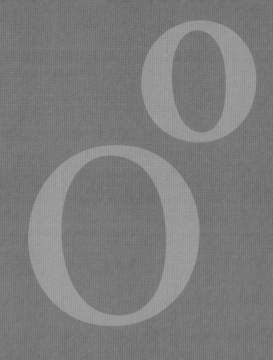

Georgia O'Keeffe was a talented artist. She fell in love with New Mexico on her first visit and said it gave her inspiration. Soon she moved to New Mexico where she painted pictures of the landscape and animal bones that were bleached by the sun. Amazed by the light, she said, "It is never, never the same. Sometimes the light hits the mountains from behind and front at the same time...so that you have distances in layers." She also said, "If you ever go to New Mexico, it will itch you for the rest of your life."

She enjoyed visiting local Native American ceremonies and spending time on her roof looking at the stars and moon. Today many artists continue to be attracted to New Mexico and its crisp, clear light, just like Georgia O'Keeffe.

Georgia O'Keeffe was an artist
and O'Keeffe begins with an O.
She found her inspiration
when she saw New Mexico.

P p

When the Spanish explorers first saw Native American villages, they called them *pueblos*, which means towns. From that, Pueblo Indians got their name. Today Pueblo de Taos (a World Heritage Site) looks almost the same as it did when Francisco Vásquez de Coronado saw it in the 1500s. There are 19 pueblos in New Mexico and they trace their origins to the Ancient Ones. One of five languages, Tewa, Tiwa, Towa, Keresan, or Zunian, is spoken at each of the 19 pueblos. Taos Pueblo and Acoma (or "Sky City") are two of the oldest pueblos.

Many pueblo houses are made from *adobe* (uh-DOH-bee), a mixture of mud or clay with straw. It is formed in bricks and then baked in the sun to dry. Adobe keeps a house cool in the summer and warm in the winter. The style of the pueblo homes was so popular that new homes have been built to look like them. This makes the word "pueblo" also known as a kind of architecture.

P is for the Pueblo villages
from long ago and still today.
Adobe homes give shelter
with their bricks of straw and clay.

Q is almost always found
with partner letter "U."
Look closely at this city's name
and see if this is true.
AlbuQuerQue

Our largest city, Albuquerque, is in the center of the state. Old Town was founded in 1706 and named in honor of the Duke of Alburquerque. (The first "r" was later dropped.) Here you can enjoy the Spanish influence of music and song while viewing Native American arts and handicrafts. Albuquerque has many museums including the National Atomic Museum and the American International Rattlesnake Museum.

The Rio Grande (in Spanish *río* means river and *grande* means big) is New Mexico's longest river and an important source of water. It flows through the entire state on a 1,900-mile journey from Colorado to the Gulf of Mexico. New Mexico is entirely bordered by land, but you will find marine life and inhabitants of the Gulf of Mexico including stingrays, jellyfish, and other fish on display at the Albuquerque Aquarium.

If you look east from Albuquerque, you will see the beautiful Sandia Mountains. *Sandía* means watermelon in Spanish and is the color the mountains turn at sunset.

Qq

R is for our *Ristras*,
sun-dried chiles on a string.
They welcome or they warn you,
and they make your taste buds sing.

Ristra means string in Spanish. *Ristras* are vibrant strings of sun-dried chile peppers that hang near entrances of homes and restaurants. They welcome guests or warn them that dishes served inside might be spicy hot. At one time *ristras* were thought to ward off evil, but now they are used for decoration or to store dried chiles for cooking.

Chile and pinto beans (*frijoles*) are the state's official vegetables. New Mexico is America's biggest producer of chiles. The town of Hatch is known as the "Green Chile Capital of the World." Chiles can be red or green, and the official state question is "Red or Green?" It's the most frequently asked question of diners when ordering traditional New Mexican cuisine.

Rr

Santa Fe is America's oldest capital. New Mexico became the 47th state on January 6, 1912. So how can it have the oldest seat of government? It became a capital in 1610. (That's before the pilgrims founded Plymouth!) It remained the capital under the control of Spain, then Mexico, and as a territory of the United States. Santa Fe also has the highest elevation of the 50 state capitals. It is 7,000 feet above sea level. It is known for its art galleries, museums, and the world-famous Santa Fe Opera, set in an open-air theater with panoramic views of the Jémez and Sangre de Cristo mountains.

The Santa Fe Trail is famous and was an important western route in the 1800s. It was 800 miles long from Independence, Missouri to Santa Fe and brought settlers westward.

S s

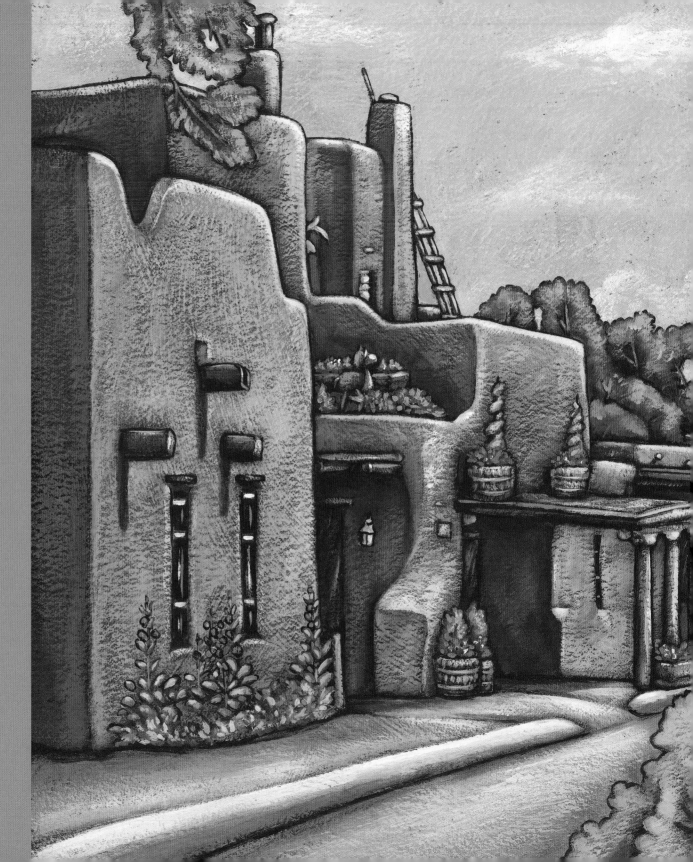

S is for old Santa Fe—
A wonderful place to vacation.
With Spanish and Mexican history,
it's the first capital in our nation.

T is also for Tourism, and you can Travel in New Mexico on many types of Transportation including a Train, Tramway, or by car on the Turquoise Trail. (Now, that's a lot of **T**s!)

If you like trains, you can take a 64-mile train ride on a 120-year-old steam train. The Cumbres & Toltec Scenic Railroad's tracks twist and turn as it travels through Colorado and New Mexico. All aboard!

At Albuquerque's edge, a tramway extends for 2.7 miles, one of the world's longest. It takes riders 4,000 feet higher in elevation in about 15 minutes as they view the deep canyons and the Sandia Mountain terrain.

The Turquoise Trail links Albuquerque and Santa Fe. On this scenic road you'll see old mining towns, tourist shops, mountain scenery, volcanic rock formations, and forests of pine and aspen.

A Train, a Tram, and a Turquoise Trail,
they all begin with T.
So take a Trip and look around
at all the sights you'll see.

In 1947 a rancher near Roswell, New Mexico, discovered unusual wreckage as he checked on his sheep after a fierce thunderstorm. The odd pieces seemed to be metal debris and they were scattered over a large area. The rancher also noticed a rut or ditch, several hundred feet long, had been carved into the land.

Some people believe it was caused by a flying saucer or UFO (Unidentified Flying Object). Others think it was a weather balloon. What do you think? The International UFO Museum and Research Center in Roswell is devoted to the Roswell Incident and UFO research.

U could be for UFOs
    with aliens—friend or foe?
Did life from far-off planets
    really land here long ago?

XING

V for *Vaquero*, the cowboy,
riding herd on his cattle and sheep.
And sometimes, of course, as he rides on his horse,
you can hear as he sings them to sleep.

Spanish explorers brought the first cattle and horses to the area in the late 1500s and started the *vaquero* (cowboy) lifestyle. In 1872 John Chisum moved his cattle headquarters from Texas and became known as the "Cattle King." Others followed, and the ranching tradition has continued from generation to generation and now includes cowgirls. Cattle drives and roundups are part of a rancher's life with long dusty days and cold sleepless nights. Cowboys sang songs to their herds to get them moving and to quiet them.

Did you know that there are more cattle and sheep than people in New Mexico? In fact, there are only 15 people per square mile. Be sure to read letters "C," "N," and "U" to learn about some interesting discoveries cowboys and ranchers made while tending their herds.

W is for this pretty Wasp,
but tarantula, beware!
That's our state's official insect
eyeing you from over there.

A classroom of students from Edgewood selected three insects as candidates for the state insect and mailed ballots to all schools for a statewide election. In 1989 the tarantula hawk wasp was chosen. This wasp stings and paralyzes tarantulas! Its bright coloring keeps it safe by warning predators that it would make a painful meal. Only a few animals eat them including the roadrunner. Maybe roadrunners think they are tasty.

The roadrunner is our state bird. It prefers running to flying and can sprint 15 miles an hour. Roadrunners are almost two feet long. They like to eat centipedes, insects, lizards, and mice. They run fast enough to catch and eat small rattlesnakes.

W
W

The word xeriscaping (pronounced zeri-scaping) comes from combining the word landscaping with the Greek word "Xeros" meaning dry. Water is a scarce and precious resource. Lakes and rivers occupy only a small percentage of the state, and there is little rainfall. The average total amount of precipitation (rain, snow, and hail) in New Mexico is 13 inches per year, but there is much less in many areas.

In xeriscape gardens, people are wise and plant native or drought-tolerant plants that need very little water. This reduces the use of water, and it requires less maintenance. This way everyone can enjoy the beautiful, unique plants of the area.

X

X can be for Xeriscaping,
an agricultural art.
Growing plants with little water
is creative and also smart.

Y y

Y is for the Yucca.
Children knew that it was great.
So they voted and decided
on this flower for the state.

Children selected yucca to be our official flower. Yucca is pretty, but it is also practical. It's kept people's hair clean for centuries. Native Americans made soap from yucca roots and because of this, it is sometimes called "soapweed." They ate the central spikes, flowers, and seedpods, and they used the leaf tip and fibers as a needle and thread.

You might be surprised to learn that the yucca's large green spears can grow to be two feet long. The plant looks like a big pincushion, and greenish-white flowers bloom from a tall stalk grown in the center. Yucca is also called "Spanish bayonet" for its long sharp leaves.

Our flag combines our Spanish and Native American heritage. The colors are from the Spanish who came in the 1500s. The Pueblo of Zia's ancient sun symbol of perfect friendship is in the center. Four rays stretch out in four directions. The Zia people believe that the giver of all good provided them gifts in groups of four. They were:

The Four Directions: north, east, south, and west
The Four Seasons: spring, summer, fall, and winter
The Day: sunrise, noon, evening, and night
Life Itself: childhood, youth, adulthood, and old age

A circle of life and love—without a beginning or an end, binds all of these.

Official Salute to the New Mexico Flag
"I salute the flag of the state of New Mexico and the Zia symbol of perfect friendship among united cultures."
Adopted March 1963

"Saludo la bandera del estado de Nuevo Méjico, el simbolo Zia de amistad perfecta, entre culturas unidas." Spanish translation adopted March 1973

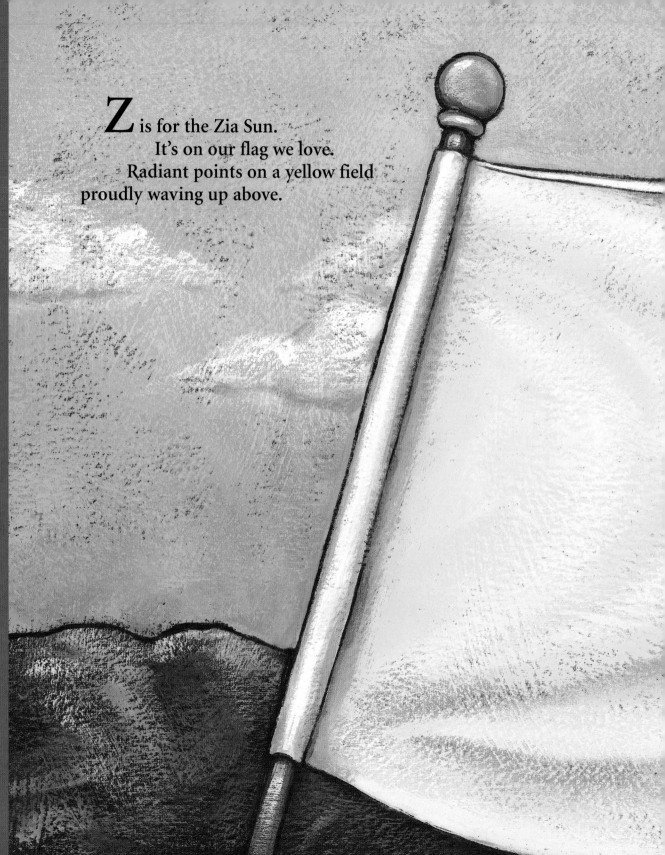

Z is for the Zia Sun.
It's on our flag we love.
Radiant points on a yellow field
proudly waving up above.

Q & A The Enchanted Way

1. What famous artist said she found inspiration in New Mexico?

2. Do you know New Mexico's capital?

3. What is xeriscaping and why is it important?

4. Who is Smokey Bear?

5. Can you name three important discoveries made by cowboys or ranchers?

6. Name some special foods you might eat when you are in New Mexico.

7. Which two official state symbols did children help select?

8. New Mexico shares an international border with which country?

9. December's birthstone is the state's official gem. What is this famous gem?

10. Why do you think our nickname is "Land of Enchantment"?

Answers

1. Georgia O'Keeffe

2. Santa Fe

3. It helps save water by landscaping using drought-tolerant plants that need very little water.

4. A little black bear cub that was rescued and became a national symbol of fire prevention

5. Carlsbad Caverns, uranium ore, and a UFO (Unidentified Flying Object)

6. Enchilada, chiles, pinto beans (frijoles), biscochito, Indian fry bread

7. Insect (tarantula hawk wasp) and flower (yucca)

8. Mexico

9. Turquoise

10. Various answers: its interesting history, beautiful scenery, wildlife, beautiful sky, views, and more

Spanish Words and Their Meanings

Adobe: Building material made of mud or clay with straw or a brick made out of the mixture

Biscochito: New Mexico's official cookie (It's also spelled Bizcochito.)

Enchiladas: A combination of sauce, cheese, chiles, onions, and meat rolled in a tortilla

Fiesta: Party

Frijoles: Pinto beans (one of the state's official vegetables)

Mesa: a hill with steep sides and a flat top

Nuevo: New

Pueblo: Town

Rio Grande: New Mexico's longest river— *río* means river and *grande* means big

Ristra: a string and also sun-dried chile peppers attached to a string

Sandía: Watermelon

Vaquero: a Spanish cowboy

Helen Foster James

Helen Foster James can hear coyotes serenade the moon from her mountain cabin. She enjoys watching raccoons, woodpeckers, wild turkey, deer, fox, and other wildlife outside her window. She has been an educator for over 20 years and is a lecturer for San Diego State University. She received her doctorate from Northern Arizona University. One of her goals is to travel to all 50 states, and she's already visited more than half. She lives in San Diego, California, in the southwest corner of the United States, with enormous stacks of children's books and her husband Bob.

Neecy Twinem

Neecy Twinem is an award-winning children's book author and illustrator with over 20 published books. Her rich, brightly colored artwork invites readers to explore the natural world. Neecy graduated with a fine arts degree from the San Francisco Art Institute, and has exhibited her artwork in the United States and Europe. After a family trip to northern New Mexico, Neecy fell completely in love with the Southwest. She fulfilled her dream to build a pueblo style home on 10 high desert acres along with her daughter, husband, two Dalmatians, two horses, and the resident wildlife. Neecy now enjoys writing and illustrating in the inspiring natural surroundings of her new home studio in the Sandia Mountains.